Developing Literacy
SPEAKING & LISTENING

PHOTOCOPIABLE ACTIVITIES
FOR THE LITERACY HOUR

year

5

Ray Barker and
Christine Moorcroft

Contents

Acknowledgements
The authors and publishers are grateful for permission to reproduce the following:
p. 11 extract from *Seriously Silly: Little Red Riding Wolf* by Laurence Anholt, first published in the UK by Orchard Books in 1999, a division of the Watts Publishing Group Limited, 96 Leonard Street, London EC2A 4XD;
p. 12 extract from 'Cinderella' from *Revolting Rhymes* by Roald Dahl, first published in Great Britain by Jonathan Cape Ltd in 1982.

Published 2006 by A & C Black Publishers Limited
38 Soho Square, London W1D 3HB
www.acblack.com

ISBN-10: 0-7136-7373-7
ISBN-13: 978-0-7136-7373-9

Copyright text © Ray Barker, 2006
Copyright illustrations © David Benham, 2006
Copyright cover illustration © Andy Robb, 2006
Editor: Lucy Poddington
Designer: Heather Billin

The authors and publishers would like to thank Fleur Lawrence and Kim Perez for their advice in producing this series of books.
A CIP catalogue record for this book is available from the British Library.

Printed and bound in Great Britain by Cromwell Press Ltd, Trowbridge, Wiltshire.

A & C Black uses paper produced with elemental chlorine-free pulp, harvested from managed sustainable forests.

Introduction

Developing Literacy: Speaking and Listening is a series of seven photocopiable activity books for the Literacy Hour. Each book provides a range of speaking and listening activities and supports the teaching and learning objectives identified in *Curriculum Guidance for the Foundation Stage* and by the Primary National Strategy in *Speaking, Listening, Learning: working with children in Key Stages 1 and 2.*

Speaking and listening skills are vital to children's intellectual and social development, particularly in helping them to:

- develop creativity;
- interact with others;
- solve problems;
- speculate and discourse;
- form social relationships;
- build self-confidence.

The activities in this book focus on the following four aspects of speaking and listening:

- **Speaking:** being able to speak clearly; developing and sustaining ideas in talk
- **Listening:** developing active listening strategies; using skills of analysis
- **Group discussion and interaction:** taking different roles in groups; working collaboratively; making a range of contributions
- **Drama:** improvisation; working in role; scripting and performing; responding to performances

Using the activity sheets

The materials show how speaking and listening can be relevant to all parts of literacy lessons, in whole-class work, in group or paired work, during independent work and in plenary sessions. The activities encourage the inclusion of all learners, since talking and contributing to group work are often more accessible than writing for lower-achieving children and for those who speak English as an additional language.

Extension activities

Most of the activity sheets end with a challenge (**Now try this!**), which reinforces and extends the children's learning and provides the teacher with an opportunity for assessment. These more challenging activities might be appropriate for only a few children; it is not expected that the whole class should complete them. For most of the extension activities, the children will need a notebook or a separate sheet of paper.

Organisation

Few resources are needed besides scissors, glue, word banks and simple dictionaries. Access to ICT resources – computers, video, tape recorders – will also be useful at times. To help teachers select appropriate learning experiences for their pupils, the activities are grouped into sections within the book. The pages need not be presented in the order in which they appear, unless stated otherwise. The sheets are intended to support, rather than direct the teacher's planning.

Brief notes are provided at the bottom of each page, giving ideas and suggestions for making the most of the activity sheet. They may include suggestions for a whole-class introduction, a plenary session or follow-up work. These notes may be masked before photocopying if desired. More detailed notes and suggestions can be found on pages 6–8.

Effective group work

Many of the activities involve children working in groups. Here are some ideas to consider as you prepare for group work.

Before you start

> **HOW?**
> - How are deadlines and groupings made clear to groups?
> - How might different children undertake different tasks?
> - How will you organise time and space to give children the opportunity to rehearse and practise new skills?
> - How will the children reflect on what they have learned about talk and its impact?
>
> **WHEN?**
> - When is working in a group appropriate?
> - When is speaking and listening to be the focus of an activity?
> - When is speaking and listening the outcome?
> - When is it right for one child to become 'an expert' and inform others?
>
> **WHERE?**
> - Where in the class is the work going to take place in order to give space and manage noise levels?
> - Where is it best for you to be to monitor the groups?
> - Where might group work result in a finished product, such as a leaflet, and what resources will you need?

Tips for grouping children

- Be clear about the nature and purpose of the task.
- Decide which type of grouping is best for your purpose (pairs, attainment groups, friendship groups).
- Consider the advantages of mixed- or single-sex groupings in your particular class.
- Consider how you will include all abilities in these groups.
- Think carefully about who will lead groups and how you can vary this.
- Aim to vary the experience for the children: for example, using different groupings, ways of recording or learning environments. Experiment with what works best for different kinds of learners.

Your role

The notes in this book suggest an active role for you as a teacher, and give examples of how you can develop children's learning. Your role will vary from activity to activity, but here are some general points to bear in mind when working with children on speaking and listening activities:

- Be challenging in your choice of topics.
- Don't be afraid to use the correct language for talk: for example, *dialogue, gesture, narrator, negotiate, open and closed questions* and so on.
- Set the ground rules: everyone has a right to speak but everyone also has a duty to listen to others, take turns and so on.
- Move around to monitor what is happening in the groups. You can move on group discussions by developing and questioning what the children say.
- Provide models of the patterns of language expected for particular kinds of speech.
- Try to steer children away from using closed questions.
- Ensure children give extended answers and always ask them to explain their thinking.
- Allow children time to formulate their responses and treat everyone's responses with respect – but avoid praising every answer.

Assessment

An assessment sheet is provided on page 48 for children to assess their own progress. The children can complete the sheet on their own or in discussion with you. It is not expected that you will be able to assess the entire class at any one time. It is best to focus on a small group of children each week, although whole-class monitoring may be possible with certain activities, such as drama activities where children perform to the whole class.

Other activities in the book are ideal for the collection of evidence over the year (for example, *The way you tell it, Tell me about yourself, And now the news…, The fear factor, Raise that cash, How does it feel?*) and for children to assess one another's skills in speaking and listening (*Get your facts straight, School dinners: 1 and 2, In trouble!, Open or closed?, The fear factor, Sort it out!, Aladdin playscript*). All the information should be assimilated for an end-of-year summary to facilitate target setting and the transition to Year 6.

Speaking

The activities in this section encourage the children to use a range of oral techniques, such as speaking persuasively and holding their audience's attention through style of delivery. There are opportunities to tell stories using cue cards, plan and carry out interviews and present spoken arguments.

The way you tell it and **Give us a cue** (pages 9 and 10). These pages provide an opportunity for the children to prepare for telling a joke, first by annotating a passage and then by making notes on cue cards. Model how to underline important words, and explain storytelling techniques such as pausing for dramatic effect. During the plenary, talk about how successful the retellings were, focusing on whether the speaker spoke clearly and made eye contact with the audience, and whether the retelling was interesting and funny.

In the deep dark wood... (page 11). For this activity it may be helpful to revise aspects of story structure such as characters, setting and dialogue. Also discuss how humour is created in the story opening. The children should be encouraged to comment on one another's performances in the plenary session.

Gory story (page 12). You could talk about other Roald Dahl stories or poems that the children know, analysing what makes them funny and interesting (for example, they never end in the way you expect).

Tell me about yourself (page 13). Here the children plan and carry out an interview. You could use this opportunity to introduce open and closed questions (see page 24); let the children question you to help them understand the difference between open and closed questions. It will be helpful to discuss how an interview might be structured to prompt the children to think about the order in which they will ask their questions.

Staff interview (page 14). This builds on the previous activity by focusing on the order of questions in an interview. You may wish to arrange for different groups of children to interview different people, resulting in a class portfolio of information on the people who work in your school. Allow opportunities for the children to talk to the class about the person they interviewed. They may wish to reorganise their notes for their talk. As a follow-up, the children could plan an interview with a famous person.

Plastic is fantastic! (page 15). This activity focuses on preparing points for an argument. The children can then go on to plan and present a spoken argument to the class. Ensure that the children have access to books and the Internet for researching the topic. Remind them that when giving a persuasive argument they need to present their points in a sensible order, use evidence to back up their points, and use persuasive language. During the plenary, weigh up the advantages and disadvantages of plastic bags and model how to construct an argument using these facts.

Get your facts straight (page 16). This activity looks at persuasive evidence, encouraging the children to explain why some pieces of evidence are more persuasive than others. As a follow-up, they could develop an argument to persuade people not to smoke, using the evidence they have chosen and the phrases on page 20.

School dinners: 1 and 2 (pages 17–18). These pages help the children to plan a spoken argument as a group. You could read the comments on page 17 with the whole class, and discuss how persuasive they are. Model how to underline or highlight the key arguments, giving suggestions for how these can be countered.

Here comes the circus and **Be persuasive** (pages 19 and 20). Here the children present an argument using persuasive language. You could make a classroom poster of the words and phrases on page 20 so that they can be used by the children whenever they have to speak or write persuasively. This links with sentence-level work on connectives. Following the planning activity, hold the 'town council meeting', inviting groups to give their speeches for and against the circus. You could vote at the end on whether the circus should be banned.

Listening

These activities encourage sustained listening, focusing on how language varies according to context and purpose, the impact of different question types, and the use of persuasive language.

Speaking slang (page 21). This activity helps to highlight the difference between formal and informal language and when each is appropriate. Discuss that different groups of people use different slang words, and that new words are always being brought into use.

In trouble! (page 22). Here the children are encouraged to report situations in different ways to illustrate how language changes according to context. This links closely with text-level work on appropriate language in writing. Invite children to perform their speeches to the class, and discuss features of formal and informal language, such as abbreviations, slang and standard and non-standard English. Children who completed the extension activity could also perform their role-plays to the class.

And now the news... (page 23). In this activity the children watch an informal news report and a more formal one, commenting on the differences. It may be helpful to highlight examples of passive verbs and slang on the activity sheet ('was rescued', 'fed up', 'great'). During the plenary, discuss the differences between the two news reports and the reasons for them, with reference to audience and purpose.

Open or closed? (page 24). Here the children learn to recognise open and closed questions. The open questions are B, E, F, H, J. The closed questions are A, C, D, G, I. Attempting to answer the questions will help to clarify the distinction between the two types of questions.

Interesting interviews (page 25). This looks at the impact of closed questions in an interview situation. You could do more work in class showing how closed questions are unhelpful when trying to encourage people to give expansive answers.

Effective questions (page 26). It is important to ensure that the children understand the different types of questions, so you will need to discuss the examples on the activity sheet. You may find the following explanations helpful:

A **closed question** is answered with a single word or a short phrase. The questioner knows what kind of answer to expect.

An **open question** may ask the respondent to reflect and give their opinions and feelings. There is no 'correct' answer.

A **leading question** is one where the questioner tries to guide the respondent's answer.

A **negative question** makes the respondent feel negative. Questions can be negative as a result of words they contain: for example, the word 'problem' in the question 'What problems keep you awake at night?'

When listening to interviews and making notes about how the questions were answered, the children should consider whether the answers were long or short, and what they revealed about the interviewee.

No answers needed (page 27). This activity looks at rhetorical questions and leads on to work on persuasive language (see pages 15–20 and 28). The children may find this concept difficult so you may wish to spend time comparing rhetorical and non-rhetorical questions, explaining their different purposes.

Sell that! (page 28). This focuses on how adverts attempt to persuade their audience. Remind the children of examples of persuasive language (see page 20). During the plenary, discuss any difficulties the children had in distinguishing opinions from facts, drawing out that adverts may present opinions as facts in order to sound more persuasive. Allow time for groups who completed the extension activity to perform their adverts to the class.

Group discussion and interaction

These activities deal with how groups interact, looking at ways of working as a group to prepare oral presentations and reach decisions. The children learn how to manage different group roles, listen constructively and achieve compromise.

Soap opera challenge: 1, 2 and 3 (pages 29–31). This group task should be carried out over a number of lessons. It links with text-level work on audience, character, plot and setting. Make enough copies of pages 29 and 30 for the children to refer to, and make one copy of page 31 per group. To introduce the activity, ask the children about soap operas they have seen on television, discussing what happens in them and what makes them different from other kinds of programmes or stories. Make it clear how long the children have to complete the challenge.

The first stage of planning is to decide how to carry out the challenge, allocating responsibilities to different group members. For the initial discussions the children should appoint a chairperson (to keep order and make sure everyone has their say) and a scribe (to ensure important points are noted down). Check that the children's ideas are not copied directly from established soap operas. Also ensure that each group nominates a pair of 'directors' who will oversee the work of the whole group and ensure that everyone's work fits together as a whole.

Page 30 provides a framework for recording decisions about the soap opera characters. The completed sheet could be photocopied for each pair in the group, so that they can refer to it as they carry out subsequent tasks.

Page 31 helps the children to carry out the paired tasks A, B and C. The children will need to come together as a group again to act out the trailer. Once the challenge has been completed, the groups should present their work to the class. Encourage each group to assess how well they organised the challenge.

Shades of meaning (page 32). This activity involves making decisions as a group. Model examples of synonyms with different shades of meaning: for example, lies and fibs. This activity could lead to some interesting work on character description: first using words with positive connotations, and then using the equivalent words with negative connotations to describe the same character.

The fear factor (page 33). This requires the children to reach decisions as a group, considering alternatives and compromising where necessary. They will need to use the language of decision-making: for example, 'Do we all agree?', 'Who disagrees?', 'Why do you think that?' and so on. The plenary session should involve assessment of how successfully the groups worked together, and how decisions were reached.

Raise that cash (page 34). The children will need to work co-operatively within the group to focus on the decisions to be made and how to reach them. You may need to handle discussions sensitively if some children have links to particular charities (such as cancer charities). If possible, hold a fund-raising day to enable the children to carry out their plans.

Holiday hints (page 35). This activity involves working together to present information in a logical way, and highlights the need for a group leader, or chairperson. Provide an opportunity for the groups to give their talks.

Sort it out! and **Listen carefully** (pages 36 and 37). These activities focus of the role of the chairperson and link to work in PSHE. Discuss with the children what they think the characteristics of a good chairperson would be.

Drama

The final section of activities looks at drama and role-play, providing opportunities to write playscripts, put on performances and use role-play to explore complex issues. The theme of several of the drama activities is pantomime – a genre with which most children will already be familiar.

The mad tea party (page 38). You may wish to begin by reminding the children that plays are written down but they are intended to be performed rather than read. The script gives the directors and actors clues about how to stage the play and present the characters. This should be developed into discussion and role-play about how the characters would move or react to the words of others. Allow an opportunity for the children to perform their scenes to the class.

Cinderella panto: 1 and 2 (pages 39–40). Here the children consider theatrical effects and how they are achieved, before writing and performing a playscript. Ensure that all the children know the original version of *Cinderella* and talk about the most memorable characters, then look at how the pantomime adapts the characters to make them comical. Allow an opportunity for groups to perform their scenes to the class.

How does it feel? (page 41). This role-play activity links with PSHE, touching on issues such as bullying and stealing which may need to be handled sensitively. The children are encouraged to explore an issue through role-play, which will lead them to appreciate that while there is no 'right answer', they can gain a deeper understanding of the problem by looking at it from different perspectives.

Put yourself in their place: 1 and 2 (pages 42–43). This links to work in history on the Victorians. The role-play activities allow the children to explore the issue of child labour from different social and historical perspectives. Discuss the historical context, explaining that children in the potteries were employed by skilled adult workers, rather than by the pottery owners. As a result, many pottery owners turned a blind eye to their ill-treatment.

Pantomime features (page 44). This activity is an introduction to the pantomime genre and its theatrical effects. It could lead in to other activities on pantomime (see pages 39–40 and 45–47). Use a video recording of a school pantomime if one is available. Alternatively, show a clip from another source, such as *The Muppet Christmas Carol* or the Blue Peter website (www.bbc.co.uk/cult/classic/bluepeter/simonpetersarah/video/video3.shtml).

Aladdin playscript, Aladdin characters and **Model theatre** (pages 45–47). This pantomime project focuses on theatrical effects and their impact. The children write a playscript and then perform it in a model theatre. You may need to draw attention to the difference between acting a performance in class and putting on a performance in a model theatre. Explain that the children may choose any episode in the Aladdin story. Once the scenes have been written and practised, allow opportunities for the groups to perform their scenes to the class, and invite comments from the audience on how effective each performance was.

How to make the model theatre:
1) Colour and cut out the theatre scenery.
2) Turn an empty shoe box upside down.
3) Glue the theatre scenery onto the base of the box.
4) Cut out the stage area from the box.
5) Cut holes in the side panels of the box so that the characters can be inserted.

How did you do? (page 48). This assessment sheet enables teachers and children to identify strengths and areas for improvement. The sheet is not intended for use after every activity, but should be given when it is felt appropriate. Sections not applicable to the activity can be masked.

The way you tell it

- **Read this joke and think about how you will tell it.**

> Underline the words you will stress.

> Mark where you will pause.

> Write ideas for adding or changing words.

> Write ideas for sound effects.

POP! BANG!

There's this <u>inflatable boy</u>, and one morning he goes to his <u>inflatable school</u> and finds himself having (a bad day.) — *a <u>really</u> bad day*

pause → Bored with the lesson, he gets up and walks out of the inflatable classroom. As he walks down the corridor, the inflatable headteacher approaches him.

The inflatable boy pulls out a pin and punctures the inflatable headteacher, before running out of the inflatable school gates. Just as he gets past the gates, he thinks, 'I hate school', pulls out his pin again and pokes it into the inflatable school. Then he runs home as fast as his inflatable legs allow, and races into his inflatable bedroom.

A couple of hours later, his inflatable mother knocks at his bedroom door, and with her are the inflatable police. Panicking, the inflatable boy once more pulls out the pin and jabs it into himself. Later on that evening, he wakes up in an inflatable hospital and, in the bed next to him, he sees the inflatable headteacher.

Shaking his deflated head, more in sorrow than in anger, the headteacher says, "You've let me down; you've let the school down; but worst of all, you've let yourself down."

- **Make cue cards to help you tell the joke.**
- **Tell the joke to the class or to your group. Use your cue cards.**

> You need the sheet called *Give us a cue.*

Teachers' note Use this with page 10; give each child one copy of each page and let the children read the joke individually or in groups (if there are children who have reading difficulties, you could put them in a group with stronger readers). Allow opportunities for the children to tell the joke to the class or a group, and encourage the audience to evaluate the performance (see page 6).

Developing Literacy Speaking & Listening Year 5 © A & C BLACK

Give us a cue

- **Cut out the cards.**
- **Make notes on them to help you tell a joke or story.**

You could make notes about:
- ☆ important words and phrases
- ☆ how you will make the story interesting or funny
- ☆ when you will pause, speed up or slow down
- ☆ when you will remind the audience what has happened so far.

Your cue cards should remind you what happens in the story, as well as how you are going to tell it.

2

1

ε

4

Teachers' note These cue cards can be used with any oral storytelling activity. Revise note-making with the whole class and remind the children that notes do not need to be written in complete sentences. Ensure that the children make notes about techniques as well as the story outline. If they need more than four cards, they can make their own by tracing around the existing ones.

Developing Literacy
Speaking & Listening
Year 5
© A & C BLACK

In the deep dark wood...

- **Read this story opening.**
  It is based on *Little Red Riding Hood*.

In the very darkest corner of the deep dark wood sat the Big Bad Girl.

The Big Bad Girl was just about as BIG and BAD as a girl can be, and all the woodland animals were afraid of her. She hung about beside the forest path and carved her names on trees. She shouted rude things at any little animal who passed by. The Big Bad Girl tripped up little deer. She stole fir cones from baby squirrels and threw them at the poor little hedgehogs. The woodland birds didn't dare to sing when the Big Bad Girl was around! But the person the Big Bad Girl liked to tease most of all was a charming little wolf cub who often passed by on his way to visit dear Old Granny Wolf.

Little Wolfie was the sweetest, fluffiest, politest little cub you could ever hope to meet. He would run along the path, skippety-skip, carrying a basket of freshly baked goodies for Old Granny Wolf, singing all the time.

From *Little Red Riding Wolf* by Laurence Anholt

The pictures show what happens in the rest of the story.

- **Make cue cards to help you tell the story.**
  Remember to use repetition and humour, like in the story opening.

> You need the sheet called *Give us a cue.*

- **Tell the story to the class or to your group.**

Teachers' note Use this with page 10; give each child one copy of each page. First read the passage to the class and talk about how it is different from the traditional tale of *Little Red Riding Hood*. If any children are unfamiliar with the original story, recap the main events. Then look at the pictures together, pointing out that the children can make up extra plot details.

**Developing Literacy
Speaking & Listening
Year 5
© A & C BLACK**

Gory story

- **Read the beginning of this poem by Roald Dahl.**

Cinderella

I guess you think you know this story.
You don't. The real one's much more gory.
The phoney one, the one you know,
Was cooked up years and years ago,
And made to sound all soft and sappy
Just to keep the children happy.
Mind you, they got the first bit right,
The bit where, in the dead of night,
The Ugly Sisters, jewels and all,
Departed for the Palace Ball,
While darling little Cinderella
Was locked up in a slimy cellar,
Where rats who wanted things to eat,
Began to nibble at her feet.

Roald Dahl

- **Make notes about what you think will happen in the rest of the poem.**

What will happen next?	What will happen at the ball?
What will the Prince do?	**How will the poem end?**

- **Retell the poem as a story. Make cue cards to help you tell it to the rest of the class.**

> You need the sheet called *Give us a cue.*

Teachers' note Use this with page 10; give each child one copy of each page. Read the poem with the children and discuss what could happen next. Allow any suggestions, encouraging the children to adapt the traditional story in any way they wish. Point out that they are going to retell the poem as a story, so it does not need to rhyme.

**Developing Literacy
Speaking & Listening
Year 5**
© A & C BLACK

Tell me about yourself

You are going to interview someone in your class to find out more about him or her.

- **Use this page to plan what you will say.**

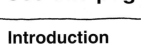

Introduction

How will you start the interview?

Questions

Who…

Try not to use questions which can be answered 'yes' or 'no'.

What…

When…

Where…

Why…

Conclusion

How will you finish the interview?

- **Carry out the interview. Record it.**

- **Listen to your interview. Did you get all the information you wanted?**
- **Make notes about how you could improve your questions.**

Teachers' note The children will need tape recorders for this activity. Ask the children to work in pairs and explain that they are going to interview their partner, each child planning their interview individually. Discuss the kinds of questions which tend to produce the most interesting responses (see also pages 24–26). During the plenary, ask the children which of their questions were most useful.

**Developing Literacy
Speaking & Listening
Year 5
© A & C BLACK**

Staff interview

- **With a partner, think of someone in your school who you would like to interview.**

We are going to interview

_____

- **Think of three main topics you want to ask the person about. Write two questions on each topic.**

Topic _____
Question _____
Question _____

Topic _____
Question _____
Question _____

Topic _____
Question _____
Question _____

- **Think about the best order for your questions. Number them 1 to 6.**

- **Carry out your interview. Remember to start and finish it properly. Make notes about what the person says.**

- **Give a talk to the class about the person you interviewed. Use your notes to help you.**

Teachers' note The children should first complete the activity on page 13. Each pair will need one copy of this sheet. Before using the activity sheet, approach people who work in the school to ask if they are willing to be interviewed. If tape recorders are available, the children could record their interviews and make notes when playing it back.

Developing Literacy
Speaking & Listening
Year 5
© A & C BLACK

• **Read this poster about the advantages of plastic bags.**

PLASTIC IS FANTASTIC!

Plastic bags have many advantages over paper bags:

1 They are cheaper to make.

2 They are stronger.

3 They are lighter.

4 They don't lose their strength when wet.

5 They are easy to re-use.

6 They occupy less land-fill space than paper bags.

7 They don't waste any trees.

• **With a partner, think of five arguments against the points on the poster.**

What are the disadvantages of plastic bags? Why might paper bags be better?

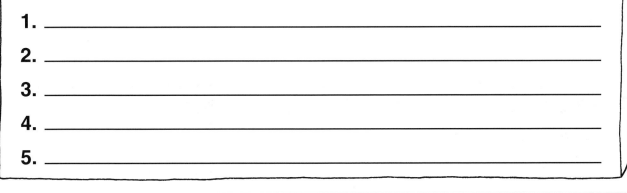

1. _____

2. _____

3. _____

4. _____

5. _____

Now try this!

• **Work with a partner. Plan an argument to present to the class about whether people use too many plastic bags.**

Teachers' note Give each pair one copy of this page. With the whole class, read the information on the poster and explain any difficult concepts. Discuss the fact that if people throw away too many bags – plastic or paper – this causes problems for the environment. The phrases on page 20 could be used in conjunction with the extension activity.

Developing Literacy
Speaking & Listening
Year 5
© A & C BLACK

Get your facts straight

When you present an argument, you need to use evidence to back up the points you make.

- With a partner, cut out the statements below.
- Imagine you are planning an argument to persuade people not to smoke.
- Choose four statements that you would use as evidence in your argument.

Which statements do you <u>think</u> contain true facts?
Which ones will help to persuade your audience?

Around half of all cigarette smokers will eventually die of an illness linked to smoking.	Smoking stops you having children. My uncle smokes and he hasn't got any children.
People who smoke get wrinkles. Most smokers look 20 years older than they really are.	One person who smoked died at the age of 38.
If you smoke, you are putting hundreds of different chemicals into your body.	Low tar cigarettes are no safer to smoke than ordinary cigarettes.
Smoking causes approximately 120,000 deaths in the UK each year. That's about 330 per day.	Cigarette smoke smells horrible. Smokers have fewer friends than non-smokers.

- **Compare your choices with another pair.**
- **Explain why you chose the statements you did.**

Teachers' note Give each pair a copy of this sheet. Discuss that points in an argument need to be backed up with evidence, and that this should be based on known facts rather than personal experience or opinions. Explain that some of the statements may not be true, so the children will need to decide which ones are plausible as well as which are most persuasive.

Developing Literacy
Speaking & Listening
Year 5
© A & C BLACK

School dinners: 1

- **Read these comments from a website discussion forum.**

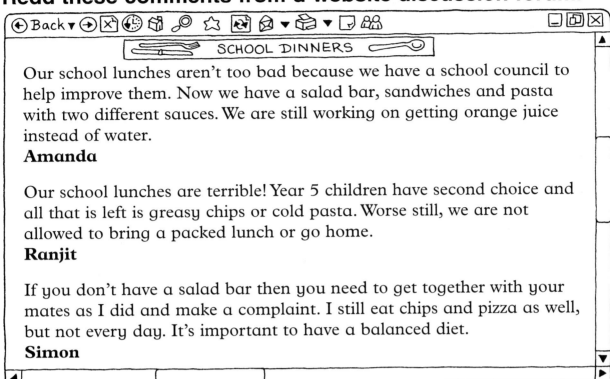

Back ▾

SCHOOL DINNERS

Our school lunches aren't too bad because we have a school council to help improve them. Now we have a salad bar, sandwiches and pasta with two different sauces. We are still working on getting orange juice instead of water.
Amanda

Our school lunches are terrible! Year 5 children have second choice and all that is left is greasy chips or cold pasta. Worse still, we are not allowed to bring a packed lunch or go home.
Ranjit

If you don't have a salad bar then you need to get together with your mates as I did and make a complaint. I still eat chips and pizza as well, but not every day. It's important to have a balanced diet.
Simon

Internet

- **Work in a group. Imagine you are going to give a speech to your school council, to try to improve your school dinners.**

- **Discuss the points you will make. Make notes on the chart.**

What our school dinners are like now	What we want school dinners to be like

- **Use the sheet called *School dinners: 2* to plan your speech.**

Teachers' note Use this with page 18. Split the class into groups of four or five and give each group a copy of both pages. One child in the group should act as scribe. Ask the children to read the website comments and to discuss their own views on school dinners. They should be encouraged to give reasons for their views.

**Developing Literacy
Speaking & Listening
Year 5
© A & C BLACK**

17

School dinners: 2

- **Use this page to help you sequence points for your argument. Make notes about the points you will make.**

> Think carefully about the order.

Introduction – set the scene

Points we shall make	Evidence and examples
1.	
2.	
3.	
4.	
5.	

Conclusion – sum up your argument

- **Give your speech to another group.**

- **Ask your audience what they thought was good about your speech. Did you persuade them to agree with you?**

Teachers' note The children should use this page to order and develop the points they listed on page 17. Allow time after the planning stage for the groups to give their speeches. Ask the audience to imagine they are on the school council and to say whether or not they agree with the argument. The phrases on page 20 could be used in conjunction with this activity.

Developing Literacy Speaking & Listening Year 5 © A & C BLACK

Here comes the circus

The circus is coming to town. Some people in the town want it to be banned.

- **Work in a group.**
  Note down arguments
  for and against the circus.

Arguments for the circus	Arguments against the circus

- **Now split into two smaller groups. One group will argue for the circus. The other will argue against it.**

- **Plan a speech for a town council meeting. Use the flow-chart below to help you sequence your main points.**

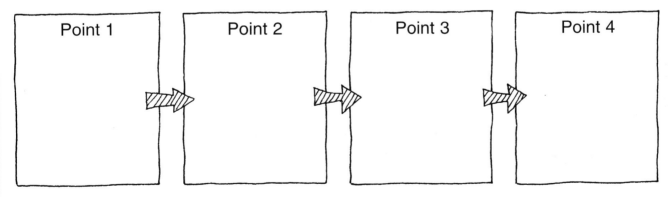

| Point 1 | Point 2 | Point 3 | Point 4 |

- **Use the sheet called *Be persuasive* to help you write sentences for your argument.**

- **Hold the town council meeting. Give your speech.**

Teachers' note Use this with page 20. Split the class into groups of four or six and give each group two copies of this page and two copies of page 20. (Each group will need to fill in two copies of the first chart.) Introduce the topic with the whole class, discussing why some people might be opposed to a circus which involves animals. Encourage the children to structure their argument carefully.

Developing Literacy
Speaking & Listening
Year 5
© A & C BLACK

Be persuasive

- **Cut out the cards.**
- **Choose four phrases to use in an argument.**
- **Think about how you will finish each sentence. Write it on the card.**

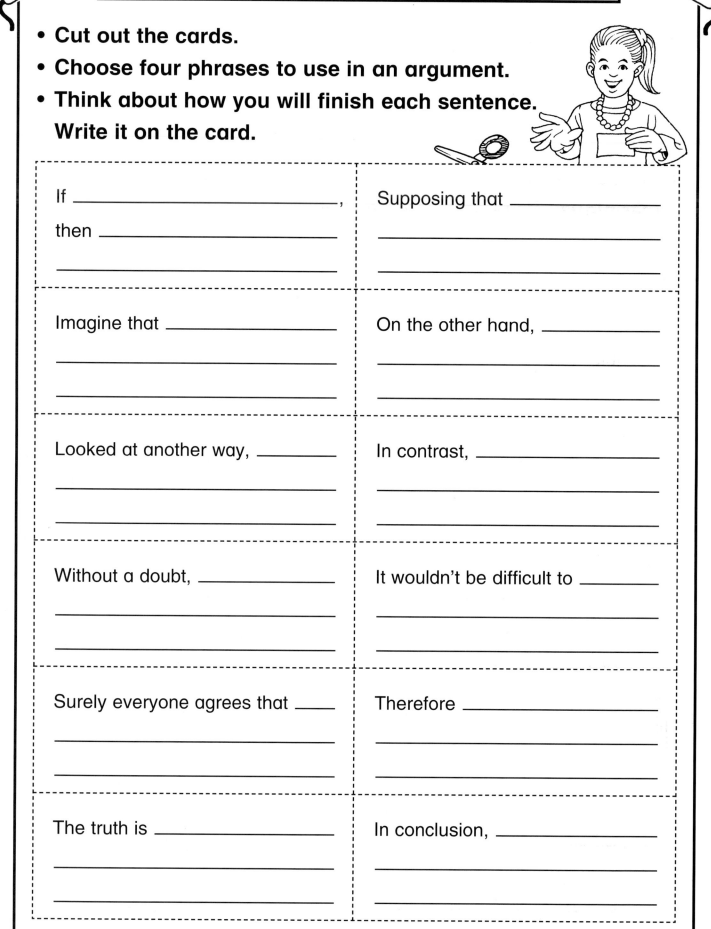

If _____,

then _____

_____

Supposing that _____

_____

_____

Imagine that _____

_____

_____

On the other hand, _____

_____

_____

Looked at another way, _____

_____

_____

In contrast, _____

_____

_____

Without a doubt, _____

_____

_____

It wouldn't be difficult to _____

_____

_____

Surely everyone agrees that ____

_____

_____

Therefore _____

_____

_____

The truth is _____

_____

_____

In conclusion, _____

_____

_____

Teachers' note Use this with page 19. It can also be used in conjunction with other activities where persuasive language is to be used (see pages 15–18 and 28).

**Developing Literacy
Speaking & Listening
Year 5
© A & C BLACK**

Speaking slang

- **Slang is used in** informal **conversations.**

Do you want a cuppa?

Cheers, mate.

- **With a partner, think of slang words which have these meanings. Write them next to each one.**

excellent _____	difficult _____
money _____	trouble _____
lots of _____	unfair _____
horrible _____	to steal _____
to fail _____	to relax _____

- **Take it in turns to choose a slang word and say a sentence using it. Then say a sentence that uses the standard English word.**
- **Your partner should describe a situation in which you might use each sentence.**
- **Make a list of situations in which you would <u>not</u> use slang.**

I would not use slang…

Hiya, Maj!

Now try this!

- **With your partner, write a slang dictionary. Find a slang word for each letter of the alphabet.**

Teachers' note Give each pair a copy of this sheet. First discuss why people use slang and in what situations. Ask the children to give examples of where they have heard slang used, in real life or on television. Talk about when the children would *not* use slang (in certain places or with certain people), and why.

**Developing Literacy
Speaking & Listening
Year 5
© A & C BLACK**

In trouble!

- **Imagine you have been in trouble at school. Make up the situation.**

How I got in trouble at school
When
Where
What happened and why

Idea bank

I kicked a ball and smashed a window.

I did not hand in my homework.

I snapped a ruler in half.

I climbed a tree and tore my shirt.

You are going to explain what happened and why.

- **Choose one of these people to explain to. Think about whether you will use formal or informal language.**

Parent or guardian

Friend

Headteacher

- **Now work in a group.**
- **Give your explanation. Ask your group to decide who they think you are explaining to.**
- **Ask your group how they could tell.**

Now try this!

- **Work with a partner. Role-play a conversation with your headteacher where you use** informal **language.**

How will the headteacher react?

Teachers' note Discuss that different situations call for different kinds of language – formal or informal. The children should work in groups of four to six. You could write the three choices (parent or guardian/ friend/headteacher) on slips of paper and put them in a bag; ask each child to draw from the bag to determine who they will be explaining to.

Developing Literacy Speaking & Listening Year 5 © A & C BLACK

And now the news...

- **Watch a formal news report and an informal one.**
- **Make notes on the chart to show the differences.**
  Give examples from the news reports.

> This morning a black and white cat was rescued from a tree in north Oxford...

> Are you fed up with exams? Well, schoolchildren in Glasgow have found a great new way to revise...

	Formal news report	Informal news report
Does the speaker use gestures?		
Does the speaker make jokes?		
Does the speaker use the word 'you'?		
Is the tone of voice friendly?		
Is slang used?		
Are passive verbs used?		
Is the vocabulary complicated?		

Now try this!

- **Work with a partner. List any other differences you noticed between the news reports.**
- **Discuss the audience and purpose of each news report.**

Teachers' note Before the lesson, record a national television news report (formal) and a children's news report (informal). Talk through the questions on the chart, then play the recordings and ask the children to answer the questions, giving examples from the news reports.

Developing Literacy
Speaking & Listening
Year 5
© A & C BLACK

Open or closed?

- **Read these definitions of two kinds of questions.**

A **closed question** asks for a short piece of information. The answer might be just 'yes' or 'no'.

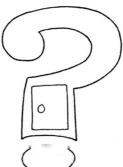

An **open question** usually has a longer answer. It may ask for an opinion or an explanation.

- **Work with a partner. Cut out the cards.**
- **Decide whether each question is open or closed. Sort the cards into two sets.**
- **Then take turns to pick a question. Read it out for your partner to answer.**

- **Check whether you have sorted the cards correctly.**

A Do you prefer tea or coffee?	**B** Why is recycling important?
C What is a noun?	**D** Is it true that all insects have six legs?
E What are your views on whether pupils should wear school uniform or not?	**F** What do you look for in a good pair of trainers?
G What is the value of 3 times 3?	**H** How do you feel when you go back to school after the holidays?
I Who is the headteacher at your school?	**J** Why is it important to learn English at school?

- **Write three more open questions and three more closed questions.**
- **Read them out for your partner to answer.**

Teachers' note First model the two kinds of questions with the children to help them understand the difference between them. Once they have sorted the cards, encourage them to answer the questions as best they can and re-sort the cards if necessary. In the extension activity, the children should check that they agree on whether the questions are open or closed.

Developing Literacy Speaking & Listening Year 5 © A & C BLACK

Interesting interviews

- **Work in a group.**
- **Choose two people to role-play this interview. The rest of the group should listen.**

> What do you find out about Robbie C?

Interview with Robbie C

Interviewer: Is it good being in the most popular boy band in the country?
Robbie C: Yes.
Interviewer: And is it true that you write all your songs in the bath?
Robbie C: No.
Interviewer: Your girlfriend told the newspapers that you were the untidiest person she had ever met. Was she right?
Robbie C: Probably.

Interviewer: What's your favourite food?
Robbie C: Bananas.
Interviewer: Do you eat these all the time when you are on tour?
Robbie C: Yes.
Interviewer: When is your next album coming out?
Robbie C: Next month.
Interviewer: So, is this the best album that you have made so far?
Robbie C: Yes.

- **In your group, discuss what is wrong with the questions.**
- **Think of five new questions which will give better answers.**

1. _____
2. _____
3. _____
4. _____
5. _____

- **Choose two people to role-play the new interview.**
- **Discuss how the interview was better.**

- **Imagine you can ask your favourite sports star three questions. Write the three questions you would ask to get the most interesting answers.**

Teachers' note Ask two children in each group to role-play the interview, or invite two children to perform it in front of the whole class. You may wish to look at some of the questions with the whole class and draw out why they are not effective interview questions. Discuss that open questions are much more useful than closed questions in an interview situation.

Developing Literacy
Speaking & Listening
Year 5
© A & C BLACK

Effective questions

- **Read these definitions of different kinds of questions.**

A **closed question** asks for a short piece of information.
Example: Where do you live?

An **open question** needs a longer answer.
Example: How does it feel to be here?

A **leading question** encourages the other person to give the answer you expect.
Example: So, this must be a very happy moment for you?

A **negative question** makes the other person feel negative.
Example: What problems keep you awake at night?

- **Listen to someone carrying out an interview.**
- **On the chart, write examples of different kinds of questions. Make notes about how they were answered.**

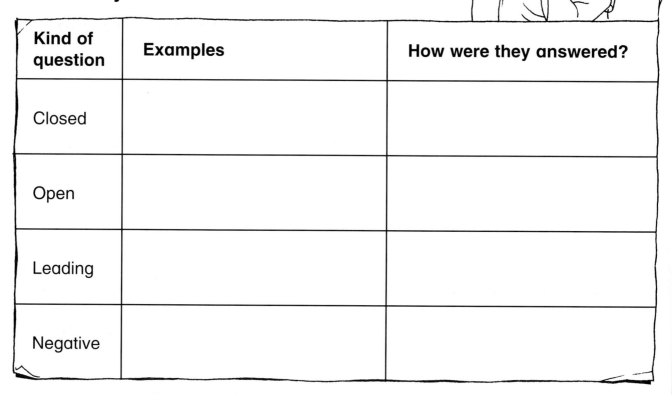

Kind of question	Examples	How were they answered?
Closed		
Open		
Leading		
Negative		

- **Discuss with a partner which kinds of questions had the most interesting answers.**

Teachers' note The children should first complete the activity on page 24. For this activity they need to listen to an interview, either recorded or live. This can be done in conjunction with speaking activities in this book (see pages 13 and 14), so that some children carry out interviews while others listen. Ensure that the children understand the different kinds of questions (see page 7).

Developing Literacy
Speaking & Listening
Year 5
© A & C BLACK

No answers needed

- **Work with a partner. Take turns to ask each other one of these questions.**
- **Answer the questions as best you can.**
- **Discuss why the answers are strange.**

Why can't everyone just get on with each other?

Why should we put up with all this litter on our streets?

Will this lesson never end?

What is the point of having a mobile phone if you never use it?

Jenny is 16 and homeless. How would you like to be in her position?

How many times do I have to tell you not to bite your nails?

- **A** rhetorical question **does not need an answer. You can use rhetorical questions when you want to be persuasive.**
- **Write four rhetorical questions of your own.**

Will _____ _____ ?

How _____ _____ ?

What _____ _____ ?

Can _____ _____ ?

Now try this!

- **Imagine you want to persuade a friend to join an after school club with you. Write down three rhetorical questions that you could use.**
- **Read your questions to your partner. Ask your partner how persuasive they were.**

Teachers' note Give each child a copy of this sheet. Introduce the activity using examples of rhetorical questions, such as 'How many times have I told you to be quiet?' Draw out that the person asking the question does not expect to receive an answer.

**Developing Literacy
Speaking & Listening
Year 5
© A & C BLACK**

Sell that!

- **Watch a television advert.**
  Make notes about how it persuades
  the audience to buy the product.

Name of product _____

Facts in the advert	Opinions in the advert
•	•
•	•
•	•
•	•

Repeated words or phrases	Persuasive language

- **Did the advert persuade you to try the product?**
  Why or why not? Discuss it with a partner.

Now try this!

- **Work in a group. You are going to make**
  up an advert for another product.
- **Choose a product and think of a name**
  for it. Make notes about how you will
  use persuasive language in your advert.
- **Practise your advert and perform it to the class.**

Teachers' note Before the lesson, record a selection of appropriate television adverts containing a mixture of facts and opinions. Before showing the adverts, discuss the features and purpose of advertising and recap the difference between fact and opinion. You may wish to produce a display showing examples of facts and opinions as a visual aid for the children.

Developing Literacy
Speaking & Listening
Year 5
© A & C BLACK

Soap opera challenge: 1

- ## Work in a group to plan and carry out this challenge.

Soap opera challenge

You are going to invent a new family of characters for a soap opera. Your tasks are:

Task A – Plot
Write the plot outline of the first episode in which the family appears.

Task B – Setting
Write a description of the family's house and what it shows about the characters.

Task C – TV trailer
Plan and act out a TV trailer which introduces the family.

- ## Use the chart to plan what you will do. Discuss the questions on the notepad to help you.

How we will carry out the challenge

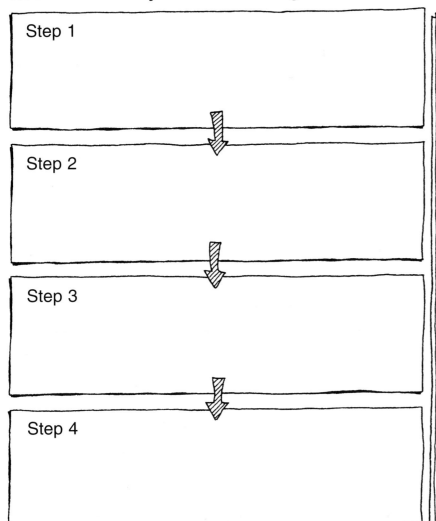

Step 1

Step 2

Step 3

Step 4

Questions
- ☆ What will the new characters be like?
- ☆ Who is the audience of the soap opera (children, adults or a mixture)?
- ☆ Who will do which tasks?
- ☆ How will everyone know what the others are doing?
- ☆ How long will the challenge take?
- ☆ How will we record our decisions?
- ☆ How will we present our work?

Teachers' note Use this with pages 30 and 31. Introduce the challenge (see page 7), then split the class into groups of eight, so that pairs of children can carry out tasks A, B and C, and another pair can be 'directors' and oversee the whole group. (If there are smaller groups, they need not carry out all of the tasks.)

**Developing Literacy
Speaking & Listening
Year 5
© A & C BLACK**

Soap opera challenge: 2

- Use this page to help you plan the new family of characters. You could use the picture for ideas.

The _____ family

Character's name	Age	Appearance	Personality	Things he or she might say

- Now decide what hobbies or jobs your characters have. Think about how these will match their personalities.

Teachers' note Use this with pages 29 and 31. This sheet should be used once the children have completed the initial planning stage on page 29. A chairperson should be appointed to make sure that everyone has their say and decisions are made as a group. One child should act as scribe and record the group's ideas on the chart.

Developing Literacy
Speaking & Listening
Year 5
© A & C BLACK

Soap opera challenge: 3

Task A – Plot

- **Plan the first episode in which the family appears.**
  Draw your own flow-chart and make notes on it.

| **Beginning** How will the episode start? Make it exciting. | → | **Middle** What will happen next? | → | **Ending** Make sure the audience will want to watch the next episode. |

Task B – Setting

- **Make notes for your description of the family's house. You could also draw pictures.**

What kind of house will it be? Where will most of the action happen?

What will the children's bedrooms be like? Think about their hobbies.

Will the family have a garden? Will they have pets?

Task C – TV trailer

- **Make notes for your TV trailer which introduces the family. Then practise acting it out.**

How will you introduce the characters? Will you have a narrator?

What will the characters do and say?

How will you make the trailer exciting? Will you use sound effects?

Teachers' note Use this with pages 29 and 30. This sheet is intended to aid the children as they carry out tasks A, B and C of the challenge, outlined on page 29. Each group will need one copy of the sheet; they should cut along the dotted lines and distribute the appropriate sections to the pairs carrying out each task.

Developing Literacy
Speaking & Listening
Year 5
© A & C BLACK

Shades of meaning

- **Work in a group. Cut out the cards.**
- **Match pairs of words that could mean the same thing.**

Use a dictionary or thesaurus.

- **Look at each pair of words. Try to agree on how the meanings are different. Use the words in sentences to help explain your ideas.**

cowardly	enthusiast	fame
fanatic	fibs	persistent
flattery	foolhardiness	frown
harsh	heroism	lies
notoriety	obstinate	praise
sarcasm	scowl	skinny
spend	squander	stern
thin	timid	wit

In each pair of words, one word suggests a more positive meaning than the other.

- **Decide which word is more positive in each pair.**

Teachers' note Split the class into groups of four to six and give each group a copy of this page. Ensure that the children have access to a dictionary and thesaurus to check meanings. You may find it easier to allocate children with the task of finding out meanings before the group starts sorting.

Developing Literacy Speaking & Listening Year 5 © A & C BLACK

The fear factor

- **Work in a group.**
- **Read the letter. Try to agree which word is best for each space.**

The words should help to show how scary the flight was.

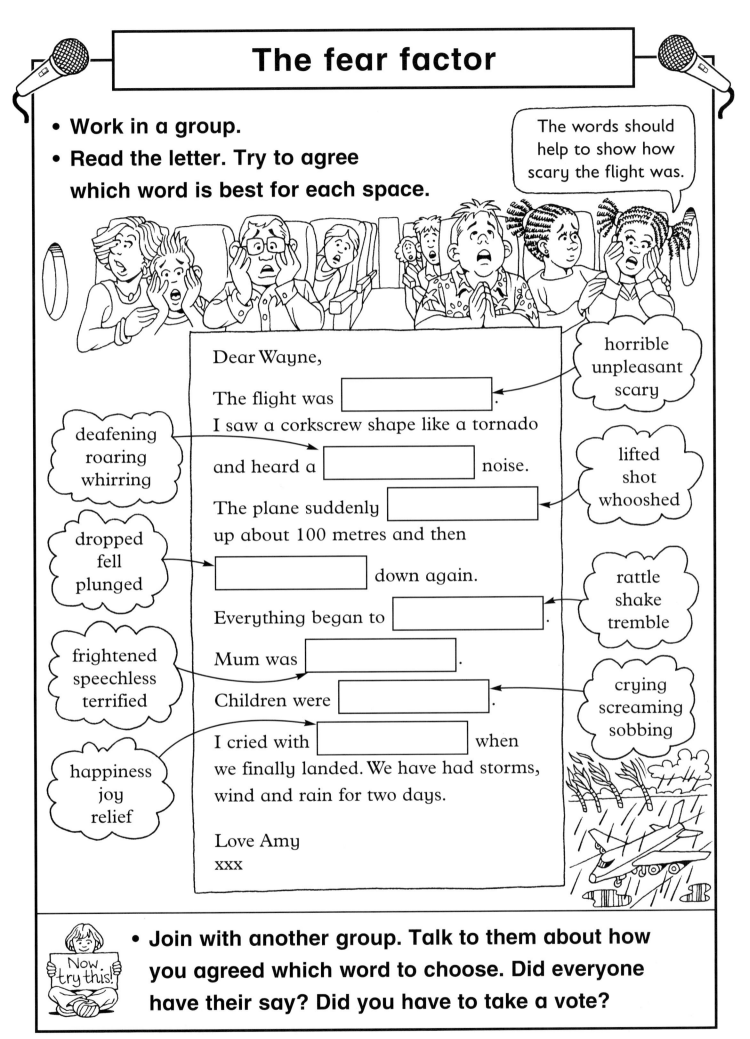

Dear Wayne,

The flight was ⬚.
I saw a corkscrew shape like a tornado
and heard a ⬚ noise.

The plane suddenly ⬚
up about 100 metres and then

⬚ down again.

Everything began to ⬚.

Mum was ⬚.

Children were ⬚.

I cried with ⬚ when
we finally landed. We have had storms,
wind and rain for two days.

Love Amy
xxx

horrible
unpleasant
scary

deafening
roaring
whirring

lifted
shot
whooshed

dropped
fell
plunged

rattle
shake
tremble

frightened
speechless
terrified

crying
screaming
sobbing

happiness
joy
relief

Now try this!

- **Join with another group. Talk to them about how you agreed which word to choose. Did everyone have their say? Did you have to take a vote?**

Teachers' note Split the class into groups of four and give each group a copy of this page. Explain to the children that there is no 'correct answer', but that it is important to give reasons why certain words are better than others in a particular context. They should try to ensure that everyone in the group has their say. They may have to vote to reach a decision.

**Developing Literacy
Speaking & Listening
Year 5
© A & C BLACK**

Raise that cash

You are going to plan a charity fund-raising event.

- **Work in a group. Use this sheet to help you plan your event. You will need a chairperson and a scribe.**

Which charity will you choose? Why?	What kind of event will you plan? How will you raise money?	When and where will the event take place?

What will you need to do before the event? How will you share out the tasks?

What will you need to do during the event?	How long will it take to organise the event?

- **Tell another group about your plans. Ask them if they think your idea will work.**
- **Think of ways to improve your plans. Make sure everyone agrees.**

Teachers' note Split the class into groups of up to six and give each group a copy of this page. Before the children begin the activity, discuss different charities and what they do. Remind them that the chairperson should be in charge of the discussion and make sure that everyone has their say. Encourage the children to achieve compromise where necessary.

**Developing Literacy
Speaking & Listening
Year 5
© A & C BLACK**

Holiday hints

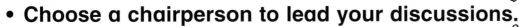

- **Work in a group. You are going to plan a talk about being responsible on holiday.**
- **Choose a chairperson to lead your discussions.**
- **Read the problems. Think of advice to holiday-makers to help solve each problem.**
- **Write your ideas on the chart.**

Problem	What to do
Many holiday resorts have water shortages.	*Take a shower rather than a bath.* *Turn off taps properly.*
Some holiday-makers waste electricity.	
People leave litter on beaches. This looks ugly and can be dangerous to wildlife.	
Cigarettes and campfires can cause forest fires.	
Wildlife is disturbed when people walk in places they are not supposed to.	
Some holiday souvenirs are made from animals which are endangered species.	
Local people sometimes complain that holiday-makers are noisy and rude.	

- **Plan how you will give your talk. Who will do what?**

- **Talk to another group about how you organised your discussions. What did the chairperson do? Did everyone join in and have their say?**

Teachers' note Split the class into groups of up to six and give each group a copy of this page. Start by asking the children where they have been on holiday, and whether they were aware of any problems caused by visitors (for example, in hot countries visitors may be asked to save water). Encourage the children to think about the role of chairperson and why it is useful.

Developing Literacy Speaking & Listening Year 5 © A & C BLACK

Sort it out!

- **Read about this family argument.**

The Kellys live in a three-bedroom house. The largest bedroom is shared by Lisa (aged 21) and Sarah (aged 10). Mr and Mrs Kelly have the second largest bedroom. Nicola (aged 18) has the smallest.

Lisa is about to move out and Sarah wants the largest bedroom all to herself. 'It's always been my room,' she says, 'and I've never had a room of my own.'

But Nicola wants the big bedroom, too. 'I'm older,' she argues. 'I need a room big enough to do my college work and have my friends round.'

The quarrel gets worse when Mrs Kelly pipes up, 'What about us? Shouldn't we have the largest room?'

- **Work in a group of four. Each person should take one of these roles:** | Sarah | Nicola | Mrs Kelly | Chairperson |

- **Discuss the problem in role.**

- **Every five minutes, change roles. Everyone should have a turn at being the chairperson.**

- **At the end of the discussion, colour the stars to show how well you did.**

★ ☆ ☆ ☆ ☆ = I need to practise this.   ★ ★ ★ ★ ★ = I did this well.

When I was chairperson:

I led the discussion effectively.	☆ ☆ ☆ ☆ ☆
I made sure everyone had a chance to speak.	☆ ☆ ☆ ☆ ☆
I listened carefully to what others said.	☆ ☆ ☆ ☆ ☆
I responded in an appropriate way.	☆ ☆ ☆ ☆ ☆

- **Discuss with your group how well you took the lead. What have you learned about being a good chairperson?**

Teachers' note Give each child a copy of this page. First discuss that the role of the chairperson is to manage the discussion, listening to others and making sure everyone has their say. Explain that this situation does not have a 'right answer', and all viewpoints should be considered by the group.

**Developing Literacy
Speaking & Listening
Year 5
© A & C BLACK**

- **Work in a group. Read this conversation.**

'Mum,' said Ranjit. 'You know that fantastic bike I'm saving up for? They've got one at the bike shop and it's on special offer. They'll take weekly payments – so that means I could have it right away and pay for it from my pocket money. It's a chance to save money, really. But you have to sign these papers...'

'I'm not sure about that,' said Ranjit's mum. 'I don't approve of having things before you can pay for them. This will mean that you are in debt and we would end up paying for it if you couldn't. I'll have to talk to your dad...'

- **Discuss what Ranjit's dad should say.**
  Choose a chairperson to lead your discussions.
- **Listen to other people and make notes about their views.**

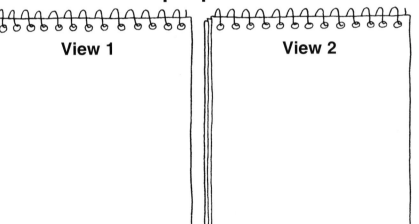

| View 1 | View 2 | View 3 |

- **At the end of your discussion, the chairperson should sum up your group's views.**

Now try this!

- **In your group, talk about how you organised your discussion. Was it a good idea to have a chairperson? Why?**

Would you do anything differently next time?

Teachers' note The children should work in groups of four. Give each child a copy of this page. Point out that the children may have different views, and everyone's opinions should be listened to and respected. Encourage the children to make notes about the different views expressed, including their own.

Developing Literacy
Speaking & Listening
Year 5
© A & C BLACK

The mad tea party

- **Read the playscript of a scene from *Alice in Wonderland*.**

- **Work in a group of four. You are going to perform the scene, using the** stage directions **to help you.**

- **First decide who will play each character. Then talk about how you will perform the scene.**

> What do the stage directions tell you about the characters?

> How will you say the words?

> How will you show how the characters are feeling?

Scene: a table set outside a house. The Hatter and the March Hare are having tea at it. A Dormouse is sitting between them, fast asleep. Alice approaches.

Hatter: No room! No room!

Alice *(indignantly)*: There's *plenty* of room! *(She sits down in a big armchair at one end of the table.)*

March Hare *(waving his arm)*: Have some wine.

Alice *(looking around)*: I don't see any wine.

March Hare *(giggles to himself)*: There isn't any.

Alice *(angrily)*: Then it wasn't very civil of you to offer it.

March Hare: It wasn't very civil of you to sit down without being invited.

Alice: I didn't know it was *your* table. It's laid for a great many more than three. *(She sulks. There is silence.)*

Hatter *(staring at Alice with great curiosity)*: Your hair wants cutting.

Alice *(severely)*: You should learn not to make personal remarks. It's very rude.

Hatter *(opening his eyes very wide)*: Why is a raven like a writing desk?

Alice *(cheering up)*: Oh, I love riddles. I believe I can guess that.

March Hare: Do you mean that you think you can find out the answer to it?

Alice: Exactly so.

March Hare: Then you should say what you mean.

Alice *(hastily)*: I do. *(Pause.)* At least, I mean what I say – that's the same thing, you know.

Hatter: Not the same thing a bit! You might just as well say that 'I see what I eat' is the same thing as 'I eat what I see'!

Dormouse *(as though talking in his sleep)*: You might just as well say that 'I breathe when I sleep' is the same thing as 'I sleep when I breathe'!

Hatter: It *is* the same thing with you. *(Silence.)*

- **Discuss how you think the scene continues.**

- **Write the rest of the scene as a playscript. Remember to use stage directions.**

Teachers' note Give each child a copy of this page and read the playscript to the children. Look at examples of stage directions together and discuss what they tell us about the characters and how to stage the play. For the extension activity, the children do not need to follow the actual events of *Alice in Wonderland*.

**Developing Literacy
Speaking & Listening
Year 5
© A & C BLACK**

- **Read the opening scene of the pantomime *Cinderella*.**
- **Work in a group. Discuss what the characters are like.**
  How does the writer make the scene funny?

Scene: the kitchen. Cinderella is dressed in rags, asleep. Her two pet mice are cuddled up with her. Buttons enters, steps to the front of the stage and looks out at the audience.

Buttons: Hello, everyone out there.

Audience: Hello.

Buttons *(putting his hand to his ear)*: I can't hear you. You can do better than that!

Audience *(shouting)*: Hello!

Buttons: That's better. Is everyone happy this afternoon? Well, we'll soon put a stop to that! So, here we are in the house of stupid Baron Hardup. He married the dreadful Sinistra and now Cinderella has been put to work in the kitchen as a slave. And I like her… *(bashfully)* … a lot! *(Shrieking is heard from the wings.)* Oh no, here comes the dreadful Sinistra. *(The Dame enters.)*

Dame: What are you doing here, you snivelling little rat?

Audience: Ooooooooh!

Dame *(moving to the front of the stage)*: And you can all shut up… *(growls)*

Audience: Booooooo!

Buttons: I'm doing my chores, madam.

Dame: What chores? *(sounds like 'What's yours?')*

Buttons: Oh thanks – mine's a cup of coffee and a chocolate biscuit! *(The Dame hits him around the head and chases him.)*

Cinderella *(waking up)*: Oh no, my wicked stepmother is bothering Buttons again. *(The two mice trip up the Dame and she falls into a vat of custard.)*

- **Decide who will play each of the three characters.**
  The rest of the group should play the part of the audience.
- **Perform the scene.**

- Improvise **the rest of the scene. Make it as funny as you can.**

Remember to use actions and gestures.

Teachers' note The children should work in groups of up to six. Give each child or pair a copy of this page and read the playscript to the children. Discuss the features of pantomime (see also page 44). When improvising the rest of the scene, encourage the children to think about how the characters would behave and react to one another. See also page 40.

**Developing Literacy
Speaking & Listening
Year 5
© A & C BLACK**

- **Read the character list from the pantomime *Cinderella*.**

Cinderella: the Pantomime

Cast of characters

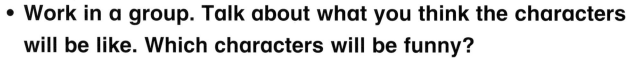

Baron Hardup	The confused and rather stupid father of Cinderella; owner of Hardup House, where most of the action takes place
Cinderella	Baron Hardup's beautiful daughter
Sinistra (the Dame)	The wicked stepmother – newly married to Baron Hardup
Gertrude and Griselda	The ugly sisters; Sinistra's daughters
Buttons	A kind servant at Hardup House; Cinderella's only friend there
Fairy Godmother	Cinderella's kind fairy godmother
Prince Michael	The handsome Prince (principal boy)
Dandini	The Prince's faithful friend
Two mice	Cinderella's pets in the kitchen (to be magically changed into footmen)

- **Work in a group. Talk about what you think the characters will be like. Which characters will be funny?**

- **Choose part of the story of *Cinderella*. Write a playscript for this scene of the pantomime.**

> Remember to use stage directions.

- **Decide who will play each part. Act the scene.**

Now try this!

- **Discuss how the stage directions helped you to act the scene.**
- **What other stage directions would be useful? Add them to your playscript.**

Teachers' note The children should first complete the activity on page 39, so that they are familiar with playscripts and the features of pantomimes. Give each child or pair a copy of this page. First discuss how the stage directions in a playscript help the actors to convey appropriate feelings and emotions when performing the scene. One child in the group should act as scribe.

Developing Literacy
Speaking & Listening
Year 5
© A & C BLACK

How does it feel?

- **Read about this situation.**

Jack is 10 and his brother Stephen is 13. Jack bought some chocolates from the local newsagent's to give to his mum on her birthday. On his way home he met a gang of older boys who stole the chocolates from him. One of the boys was his brother's friend, Paul.

Jack didn't have enough money to buy another box of chocolates for his mum, so he went back to the newsagent's and stole one. His friend Chloe saw him do it.

- **Work in a group of four. Each of you take one of these roles.**

| Jack | | Jack's mum | | Shopkeeper | | Chloe |

- **Think about these questions. Then make notes about your character's point of view and feelings.**

Why did Jack think it was all right to steal another box of chocolates?

How would Jack's mum feel if she knew Jack had stolen the chocolates?

What could Jack have done instead?

Should Chloe tell anyone what she saw?

_____'s point of view	_____'s feelings

- **In role, discuss whether Jack had a good reason to do what he did.**

- **In your group, talk about how your role-play helped you to understand the problem. Did you all agree on what Jack should have done?**

Teachers' note Give each child a copy of this page. Read the situation with the children and explain that they are going to use role-play to think about it from different points of view. During the plenary, discuss the issue of bullying and how to cope with it, with reference to what Jack could have done after the older boys stole from him.

**Developing Literacy
Speaking & Listening
Year 5
© A & C BLACK**

Put yourself in their place: 1

- **Read this extract from a report. It is about children working in the potteries in the 19th century.**

Each man employs two boys, one to turn the jigger, or wheel, from morning to night; the other to carry the ware just formed from the 'whirler' to the hot-house and moulds back. These hot-houses are rooms within rooms, closely confined except at the doors, and without windows. In the centre stands a large cast-iron stove, heated to redness, increasing the temperature often to 130 degrees. I have burst two thermometers at that point. During this inclement season I have seen these boys running to and fro on errands, or to their dinners, without stockings, shoes or jackets, and with perspiration standing on their foreheads, after labouring like slaves, with the mercury 20 degrees below freezing. The results of such transitions are soon realised, and many die of consumption, asthma, and acute inflammations.

From Mr Samuel Scriven's Report on the Staffordshire Potteries, 1843

- **Work in a group. Talk about what it would have been like to work in the potteries. Make notes on the cards.**

How would you feel on your way to work?	...when you were at work?
...when you got home?	How would you behave towards your master?

Now try this!

- **Imagine you are a boy working in the factory and you start to feel ill.**
- **With a partner, role-play a conversation between the boy and his employer.**

Teachers' note Give each child a copy of this page. If this aspect of Victorian history has not been studied, take time to discuss what the life of working children must have been like, and how their employers might have treated them (see page 8). Stress that this is a true report, and explain that the author, Mr Samuel Scriven, wanted to help change the law. See also page 43.

**Developing Literacy
Speaking & Listening
Year 5
© A & C BLACK**

Put yourself in their place: 2

- **Read these people's views.**

John

> I'm eight and I work 14 hours a day. Children like me don't go to school – that's just for rich families.

John's mother

> My youngest son works in the potteries. I don't like it, but we need the money he brings in. We have barely enough food as it is.

Pottery owner

> If my workers want to employ children, that's their business. I have a factory to run and I can't afford to be soft.

Mr Scriven

> These children risk their lives every time they go to work. We need new laws to improve their working conditions.

- **Work in a group of four. Each take one of the characters.**

- **Put yourself in the character's place. Make notes about their views and the reasons for them.**

Character

My views

Why I think this

- **In role, discuss whether there should be new laws about children working in the potteries.**

Now try this!

- **What do you think about the problem? Write a report of how this activity has helped you to develop your views.**

Teachers' note The children should first complete the activity on page 42. Give each child a copy of this page and explain that the people shown are characters from the 1840s. Encourage the children to put aside their own personal views and feelings in order to explore the issue from their character's point of view.

Developing Literacy Speaking & Listening Year 5 © A & C BLACK

Pantomime features

- **Read the passage about pantomime.**

Pantomime is a Christmas or New Year entertainment in Britain. The main characters are a principal boy and a heroine, which are both played by young women. The 'dame' is played by a man! The plot is usually based on a folk tale, such as Puss in Boots or Cinderella.

The ingredients of pantomime include slapstick comedy (such as custard pies being thrown in people's faces), popular songs and audience participation. Everyone boos the villains and there are arguments between characters and the audience. In the end, the villains get what they deserve and the good characters live happily ever after.

- **Watch a pantomime performance. Look for examples of the features on the chart.**
- **Work with a partner. Make notes on the chart.**

Name of pantomime _____

Feature	Examples from performance
Good characters	
Villains	
Slapstick comedy	
Popular songs	
Audience participation	

- **Think about how a pantomime makes you feel. How is it different from other plays? Talk with a partner and make notes.**

Teachers' note Before the lesson, obtain a video recording of a pantomime (see page 8). First read the passage with the children and encourage children who have been to a pantomime to describe what it was like. Compare this with other plays the children have seen. Then talk through the features on the chart before playing the recording. Share the children's ideas during the plenary session.

Developing Literacy
Speaking & Listening
Year 5
© A & C BLACK

Aladdin playscript

- **Work in a group. You are going to write a scene for the pantomime _Aladdin_.**

- **Read the cast list and the plot. Discuss what will happen in your scene. You do not have to use all the characters.**

The cast

Aladdin	A bright, honest peasant boy
Widow Twanky	A washerwoman; mother of Aladdin, Wishee and Washee
Wishee and Washee	Aladdin's younger twin brothers (not very bright)
Abanazer	An evil magician
Emperor	The Emperor of China
Princess So-Shi	The Emperor's beautiful daughter
Genie of the Lamp	A magical genie who can grant any wish

The plot

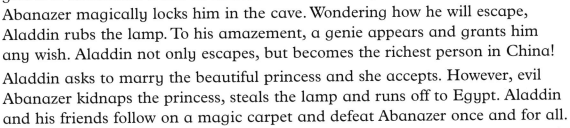

The evil magician Abanazer hears of a magic lamp hidden in a cave in China. He travels there and looks for a peasant boy who will fetch the lamp for him. Aladdin is working in his mother's laundry when Abanazer arrives and pretends to be his long-lost uncle. Aladdin goes to the cave and finds the lamp, but decides not to give it to Abanazer. When he refuses to hand it over, Abanazer magically locks him in the cave. Wondering how he will escape, Aladdin rubs the lamp. To his amazement, a genie appears and grants him any wish. Aladdin not only escapes, but becomes the richest person in China!

Aladdin asks to marry the beautiful princess and she accepts. However, evil Abanazer kidnaps the princess, steals the lamp and runs off to Egypt. Aladdin and his friends follow on a magic carpet and defeat Abanazer once and for all. Aladdin and the princess are married, and the Emperor falls for Widow Twanky!

- **Write your scene. Use the features of pantomime.**

- **You need the sheets called _Aladdin characters_ and _Model theatre_. Make the characters and the theatre.**

- **Perform your scene to the rest of the class.**

- **Discuss how successful your performance was. Did your audience react in the way you expected?**

Teachers' note Use this with pages 46 and 47. Split the class into groups of four to six and give each group one copy of pages 45, 46 and 47. First revise the features of pantomimes (see page 44) and how to write a playscript. Read the cast list and the plot together, and explain to the children that they are going to write a scene for performance in a model theatre.

**Developing Literacy
Speaking & Listening
Year 5
© A & C BLACK**

Aladdin characters

- **Colour and cut out the characters.**
- **Tape each character**
  to a drinking straw.
  Use the characters
  in your model theatre.

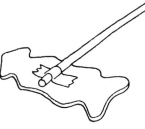
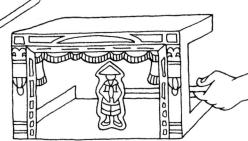

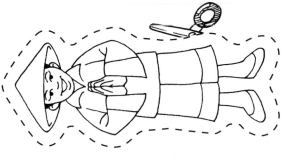 **Washee**

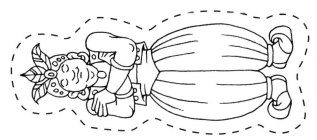 **Genie**

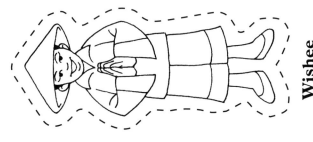 **Wishee**

 **Princess So-Shi**

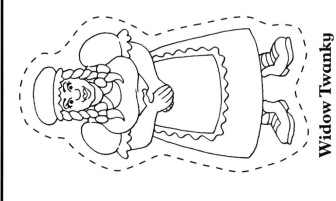 **Widow Twanky**

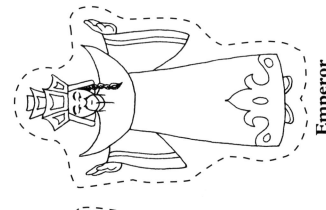 **Emperor**

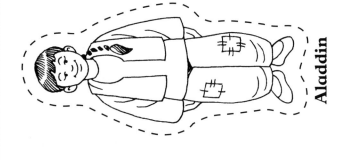 **Aladdin**

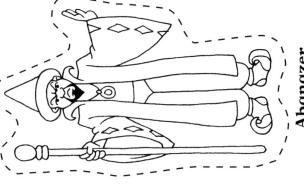 **Abanazer**

Teachers' note Use this with pages 45 and 47. Photocopy this page onto card if possible. Each group will need eight drinking straws, scissors, coloured pencils and sticky tape. The characters can be used in the model theatre by inserting them through the holes in the sides (see pages 8 and 47).

Model theatre

Teachers' note Use this with pages 45 and 46. You will need to demonstrate how to make the model theatre (see page 8). The children could make additional scenery and props.

Developing Literacy
Speaking & Listening
Year 5
© A & C BLACK

How did you do?

Name _____ Date _____

Activity title _____

When you listened to others

- **What was good about what they said?**

  _____

  _____

- **What could they have done better?**

  _____

  _____

When you spoke

- **What did you do well?**

  _____

  _____

- **What could you do better next time?**

  _____

  _____

When you talked in a group

- **What was good about your discussion?**

  _____

  _____

- **Did you have any problems? If you did, what were they?**

  _____

  _____

Teachers' note Photocopy this page and fill in the title of the activity to be self-assessed. Before the children complete the assessment sheet, you could ask them whether they enjoyed the activity, and to explain why or why not.

Developing Literacy Speaking & Listening Year 5 © A & C BLACK